LEARN TO READ WITH PHONICS

Dear parents and teachers,

This is a fast and effective way of teaching your child to read fluently, whether he or she is:

- four and ready to read,
- a reluctant reader aged nine or more,
- if he or she has a learning difficulty,
- or if English is a second language,

This reading scheme is for you.

- It is for everyone who wants to **read fast**.
- This scheme is **easy to use**.
- It uses **phonics** or sounds.

The course consists of eight reading books. Book 1 and 2 are for pre-readers. These teach initial sounds and word building with three or four letter words. Books 3 - 6 teach phonic sounds in this order:

ch, sh, wh, th, oo, ee, ar, or, ur, ir, er, magic e, ea, oa, ai, ay, oi, oy, oa, short y as in happy, long y as in sky, soft c as in mice and soft g as in engine, ou, ow, au and aw.

The final book introduces more complex sounds as in, tion, le, el, prefixes and suffixes.

There are further titles available on our website for readers who have attained a degree of fluency.

How does it work?

Each chapter introduces a sound.

1. Learn the sound with your child.

2. Read the sentences several times, encouraging your child to talk about the picture.

3. At the end of the sentences, there is a list of words and phrases, which the child can match to the pictures.

Practise each sound several times, until your child is familiar with it.

It is **important** to **practise**. Move on to the next sound and chapter when you are confident that your child has learnt all the material.

Working out words, can be done by learning the phonic sounds and then running them together.

>ch ee k y

>ar ch er y

>hun dred - has two syllables

80% of words can be learnt this way, but a few words will need to be learnt by **looking**, **saying** and **remembering** them.

Children using phonics in this way progress fast.

Dear Kids,

> LEARN TO READ, BY READING WITH SAM, KIM AND THEIR FRIENDS.

Sam

Kim

Meet Sam and his sister Kim.

They have a cat and a dog called Spot.

Next door, there are two children called Frank and Kelly. They are the best friends of Sam and Kim.

You will meet some more of their relatives and friends including: Auntie Grace, Uncle Cyril, their cousins Grace and Nancy, the famous cousin from the country, his mum and dad, and Frank's Uncle Paul, who takes the children out.

You will also meet: Kim's friend Candice, Sam's school friend Peter, who likes football, his teacher and his class mates, like Heather.

Have Fun Learning To Read.

This course may also be used for older children or adults, who have problems with reading and spelling.

Read the sentences, but concentrate on spelling the words in each chapter, progressing from easier to harder words, depending on ability.

It is as easy as that!

If you need help using the scheme, email at:
www.guineapigeducation.co.uk

Sam says, "Sweets are not good for your teeth, but it is good to swim in the pool."

Learn **ch**, **sh**, **th**, **ee** and **oo** sounds with Sam:

Read this sentence:

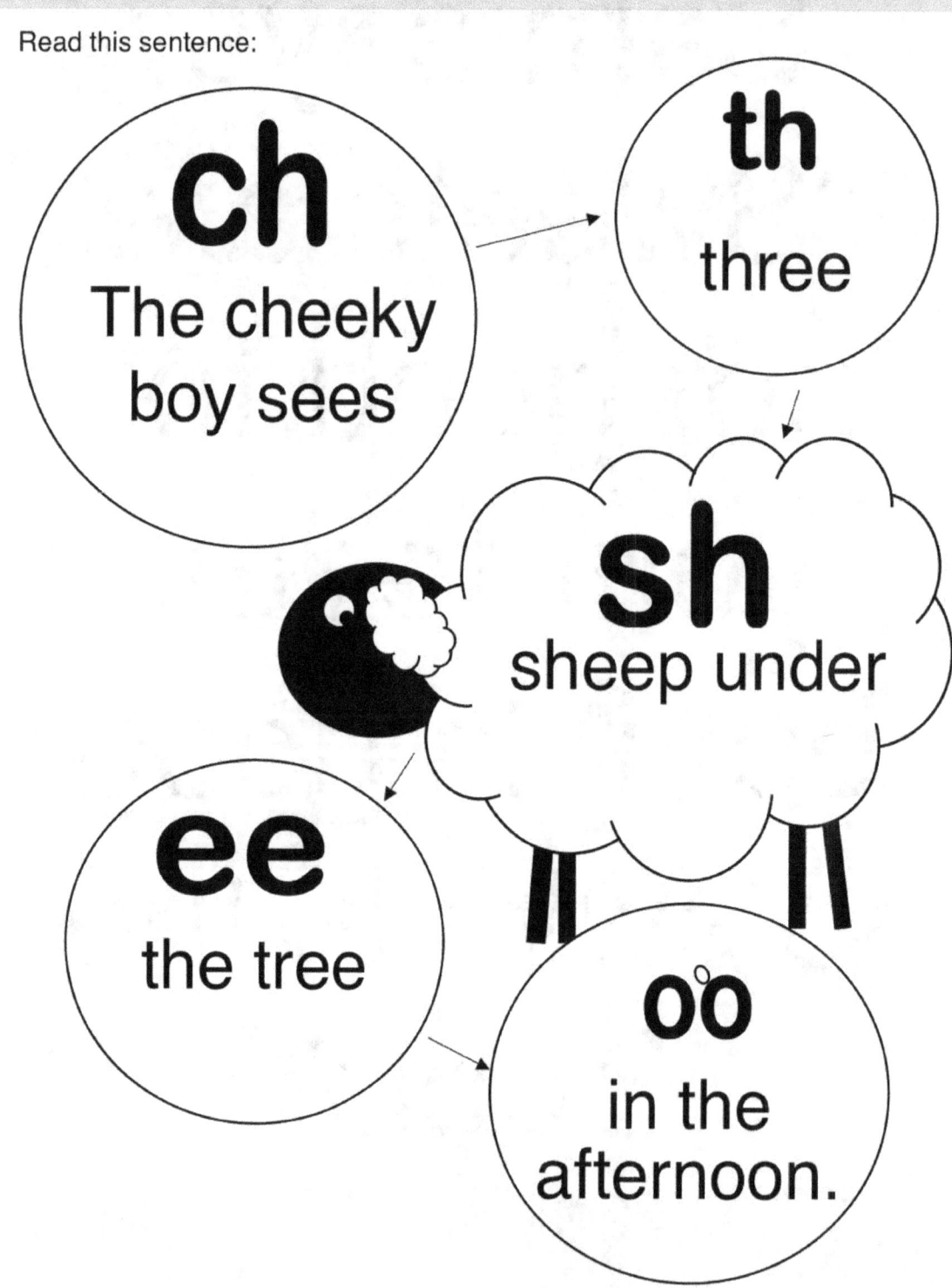

ch — The cheeky boy sees
th — three
sh — sheep under
ee — the tree
oo — in the afternoon.

Read these sentences.

Look at each page. Find words with oo, ee, ch, sh, th. You can write them in a list.

Kim likes food.

She likes fish and chips.

Kim likes fish and chips. She likes this food so much.

Kim likes sweets.

Kim likes sweets, but mum seems to think they are not good for her teeth. She does not want a bad tooth.

Kim does not want a bad tooth.

Are sweets good for Kim's teeth?

Yes or no?

The sweet shop has just shut. Kim cannot go in. She will not get a bad tooth.

Sam thinks it is good to go to the pool each week.

He thinks he swims well.

Sam feeds the cat. The cat looks at the food.

Sam spoons the cat food into a dish.

He chops the food up into chunks.

Sam is sent to bed. He has been so cheeky. Mum is mad with him.

Sam and Kim are cold and wet. Sam has a thick jumper with a hood. They run to the van and get in. Kim shuts the door.

In the week, Sam and Kim
go to see the ships with Dad.

They see the sheep under the tree.

The sheep are under the tree. They see three sheep there.

Learn these words. Cut them out and match them to the pictures on the next pages.

tree	spoon	chunk	this
good	feed	sheep	hood
seem	sweet	think	teeth
cheek	thick	green	chick
shop	see	been	shut
fetch	ship	look	week
fish	chop	tooth	food
that	pool	chips	bath
much	shop	cheeky	dish

Learn these phrases. Cut them out and match them to the pictures on the next pages.

see the ships	see the sheep
under the tree	fetch his cat
likes sweets	feeds his cat
looks for food	bad tooth
seems to think	not good for teeth
thinks its good	shop is shut
get his sweet	go to the pool
every week	been cheeky

spoons the cat food	in a dish
into chunks	chops the food
likes fish and chips	likes food
shuts the door	thick jumper
with a hood	

If you can read the words in these phrases go on to the next chapter.

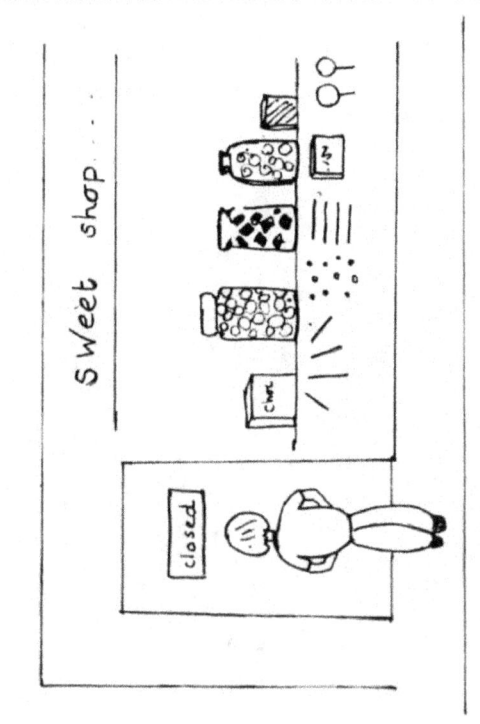

Kim likes to see the horses at the farm.

Read on to learn the sounds **or** as in horse and **ar** as in farm.

Look at each page. Find the words that have or and ar. You can write them in a list.

Ar

Sam and Kim get into the car.

Or

Sam plays with his fort.

Read these sentences.

It is the weekend. Kim and Mum have been to the shops in the van. They run to the porch to get out of the storm.

Sam likes sport. In the morning, he has a go at archery. He hits the target and scores a bullseye. He feels good about himself.

In the afternoon, he plays with his darts.

In the corner of the room, Kim sits on the carpet. She is holding her pet rabbit. She calls him darling.

Kim's rabbit nips her hand. He is having fun. "No, no, no! You are a bad rabbit," she says, "You have sharp teeth."

Kim's hand is bleeding a bit. The rabbit's teeth are very sharp. She calls mum who is in the corner of the room. "Look at my hand," she says. Mum gets a plaster.

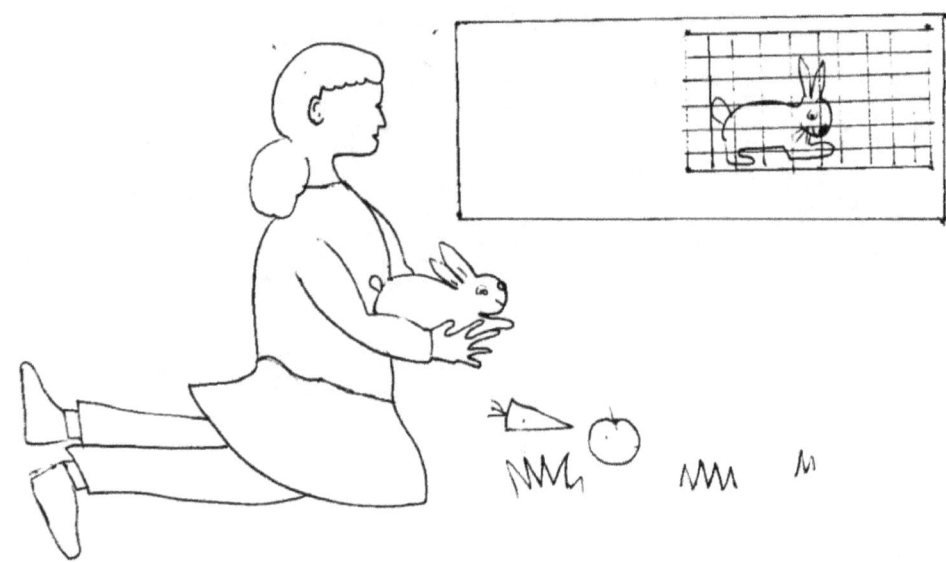

Soon the bleeding stops, Kim hugs her rabbit and puts him in his box. All is well.

Sam needs a plaster too. He has pricked his hand on a thorn.

Sam and Kim go to the farmyard with Frank who lives next door. They go to see the horses. They feed them some grass.

The farmer is not there. He is at the market this morning.

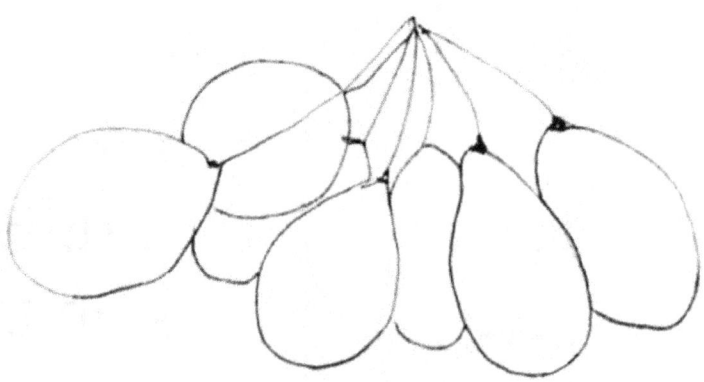

Kim looks smart. She is going to a party. It is Norma's party.

Kim must not forget the present. She gets it before she shuts the door.

Learn these words. Cut them out and match them to the pictures on the next pages.

sport	morning	archery	storm
porch	darts	target	scores
thorn	car	darling	corner
fort	carpet	sharp	farm
yard	horse	farmer	market
report	born	smart	party
forget	hard	Norma	

Learn these phrases. Cut them out and match them to the pictures on the next page.

Sam has worked hard.	sharp corner
looks smart	Norma's party
in the farm	going to a party
a good report	likes sport
run to the porch	works hard
to get out of the storm	a go at archery
hits the target	on a thorn
go to the farmyard	see a horse
a darling rabbit	her mother sits in the corner
farmer not there	at market
this morning	on the carpet
has sharp teeth	must not forget

If you know the words in these phrases, go on to the next chapter.

A balloon bursts.

Sam's cat is scared.

Look at his fur?

He sits under the parked car.

Sam teaches you **ar**, **or**, **ir**, **ur** and **er** sounds.

Read the following pages.

Look at each page and find the words with the sounds **ar**, **or**, **ir**, **ur**, and **er**.

Underline

ar words in red – as in car
or words in blue – as in fort
er words in green – as in under
ir words in yellow – as in shirt
ur words in purple – as in fur

You can write them in a list.

Read these sentences...

Sam's cat bursts the balloon that Sam got from Norma's party. It burst on a thorn in the garden.

It went off with such a bang. Sam's cat is scared by the bang. His fur stands on end.

Some postcards come from grandma and grandad. Kim's card is of a farm. There is a horse in the farmyard. There is an old barn with some hens. On the roof a black bird sings a song.

Draw Kim's postcard here.

Sam's card is of a ship. The sun sparkles on the water.

Draw Sam's postcard here.

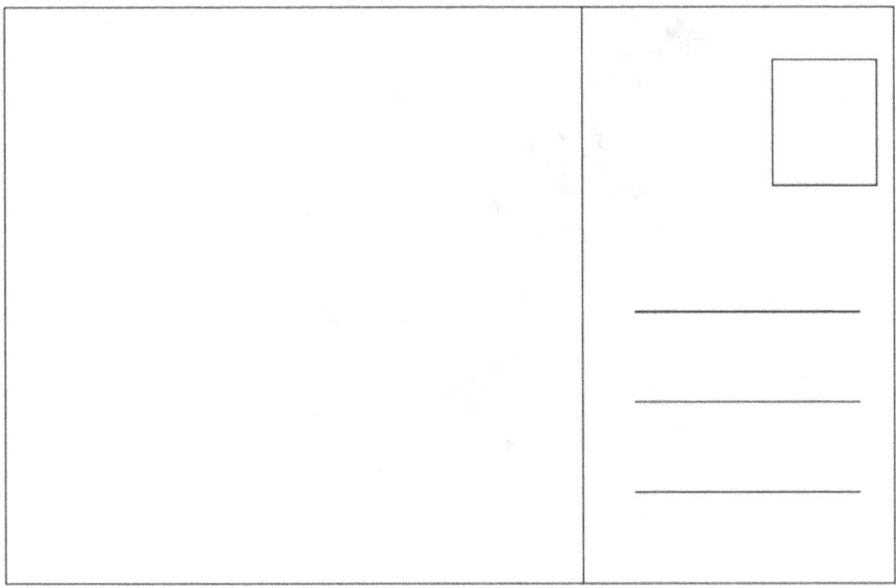

Sam and Kim like the cards. They are smart cards.
They are cool.
They are charming cards and they stick them on the bedroom wall.

Sam and Frank like sport. Sam can run faster than Frank.

They both get thirsty when they run and need a drink.

Sam is in the car with his Dad.
When he needs to turn left, he
misses the turning. They are lost.
Dad goes red because he is cross.

Then, Sam's Dad goes too fast in
the car. He jerks the car, as he
turns the corner and makes Sam
jump.

"Help me!"

This term there will be thirty children in Kim's class. Frank says that he thinks there are only twenty-five children in his class. Kim has a lot of girls in her class.
Kim's teacher is kind but she can be strict.

She says firmly to her class, that she does not want a murmur when they are reading.

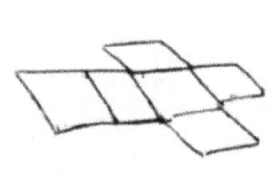

Frank's sister Kelly likes to dress up. Sam watches her. Her skirt is long, her shirt is silk and her hair is curled. She pretends she is an important person.

Kelly likes to dress up like a nurse. She nurses Sam and pulls a thorn from his finger. Sam is sad because his hand hurts, so he asks the nurse for a plaster.

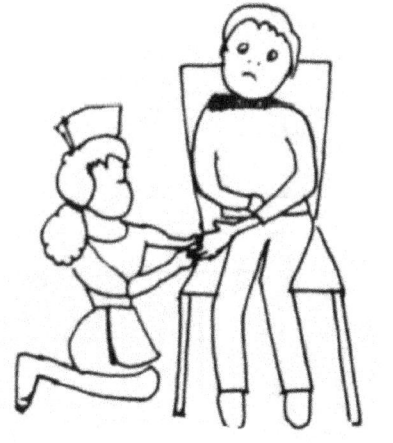

**Collect words with these sounds from the story.
Write them here.**

ar

or

ir

ur

er

Learn these words. Cut them out and match them to the pictures on the next pages.

sport	burst	barn	faster
dart	far	farm	person
murmur	thirty	charm	nurse
father	term	important	born
corner	morning	corn	sparkling
card	turn	thorn	bird
skirt	shirt	curl	jerk
firm	fork		

Learn to read these sentences. Cut them out and match them to the pictures on the next pages. A sentence has a capital letter and a full stop.

It is Norma's birthday.	The teacher is firm.
It is a charming card.	They get thirsty.
She has a silk shirt.	She says not a murmur.
She has a long skirt.	She dresses up as a nurse.
There are lots of girls.	The sun sparkles on the water.
There are thirty children in the class.	Dad jerks the car.
They turn left.	They like sport.
The birds sing.	This is Kim's teacher.
They are in the car.	The cat's fur stands on end.
Her hair is curled.	Frank runs faster.
He turns the corner.	He misses the turning.

If you know the words in these sentences, you can go on to the next chapter.

On a fine weekend Sam plays under the pine trees.

Sam teaches you to read 'magic e'.

These pages teach you 'magic e' or 'silent e', as in **cake**.

'Magic e' makes the '**a** sound' of c**a**ke into a **long** sound.

For example,

Bike

Tube

Home

Have long sounds and 'magic e'.

Read the following pages.
Underline words with a 'magic e'.
You can write them in a list.
Long a sounds in red
Long e sounds in blue
Long i sounds in green
Long o sounds in orange
Long u sounds in purple

Here are some words to look for:

Stone

Pine

Game

Read these sentences.

On a fine weekend in summer, Sam and Kim have dinner in the park. They sit on the grass under the pine trees with Mum and Dad.

They have cheese sandwiches, crisps and cakes on paper plates. The children drink lemon. Mum and Dad have a glass of wine.

The sun is hot. The sky is blue. It is pure blue. Mum and Dad relax on the picnic rug. Dad looks at his paper, while Mum chats on her mobile. Sam hits the ball with his bat and Kim catches it. Sam wants to use his kite, but there is no breeze.

Then, Dad says he will take them to the theme park next week, but they will only go if the sun shines. They have not been to Hope Park for a long time. It is open in the summer.

It is a fine afternoon. After school, Sam and Frank skate on their roller blades on the path by the flats, with their mate Peter.

The girls are there too, but they do not want to skate. They make an excuse. They hide by the gate and watch the boys on their roller blades. The boys skate fast on the concrete path. Soon the girls go off by themselves.

Sam and his mates like to play games. Sometimes they make a treasure hunt like they did at Norma's party.

Sam hides some clues in the garden. Kim, Frank and Peter look for the clues. They find the clues under the pots and stones. The last clue tells Kim that the treasure is by the gate. She finds the treasure. The prize is some sweets.

Sam hurts his toe on a stone in the garden. It hurts so much that he is jumping up and down.

Kim says, "Stop Sam! It is not as bad as you think. There is nothing there."

Frank lives next door to Sam, with his sister Kelly. They chat to each other over the wire fence.

Frank tells Sam he cannot ride his bike. It is broken. There is a hole in the inner tube. His Dad is going to take it to the bike shop, to be mended.

The small kids are having fun. Kelly likes to pretend. This time she is pretending she is a zookeeper.

In her game, a tiger has escaped from the zoo.

She rescues Kim from the tiger. She catches the tiger with a rope and takes it back to the zoo.

List the 'magic e' words here.

a – 'e'

e – 'e'

i – 'e'

o – 'e'

u – 'e'

Learn these words. Cut them out and match them to the pictures on the next pages.

fine	pine	paper	plate
wine	shines	pure	blue
theme	time	Hope	open
kite	bike	hole	tube
take	skate	mate	blade
gate	prize	treasure	game
hide	clue	rescue	tiger
toe	rope	take	escape
make	excuse	concrete	wire
fence			

Learn these phrases. Cut them out and match them to the pictures on the next pages. A phrase is part of a sentence. It doesn't need a capital letter or full stop.

hurts his toe	likes to play games
wire fence	bike shop
hole in the inner tube	make a treasure hunt
pine trees	hide some clues
fine weekend in summer	pure blue
sky is blue	glass of wine
concrete path	skate on roller blades
cakes on paper plates	hide by the gate
good game	make an excuse
rescues Kim from a tiger	with a rope

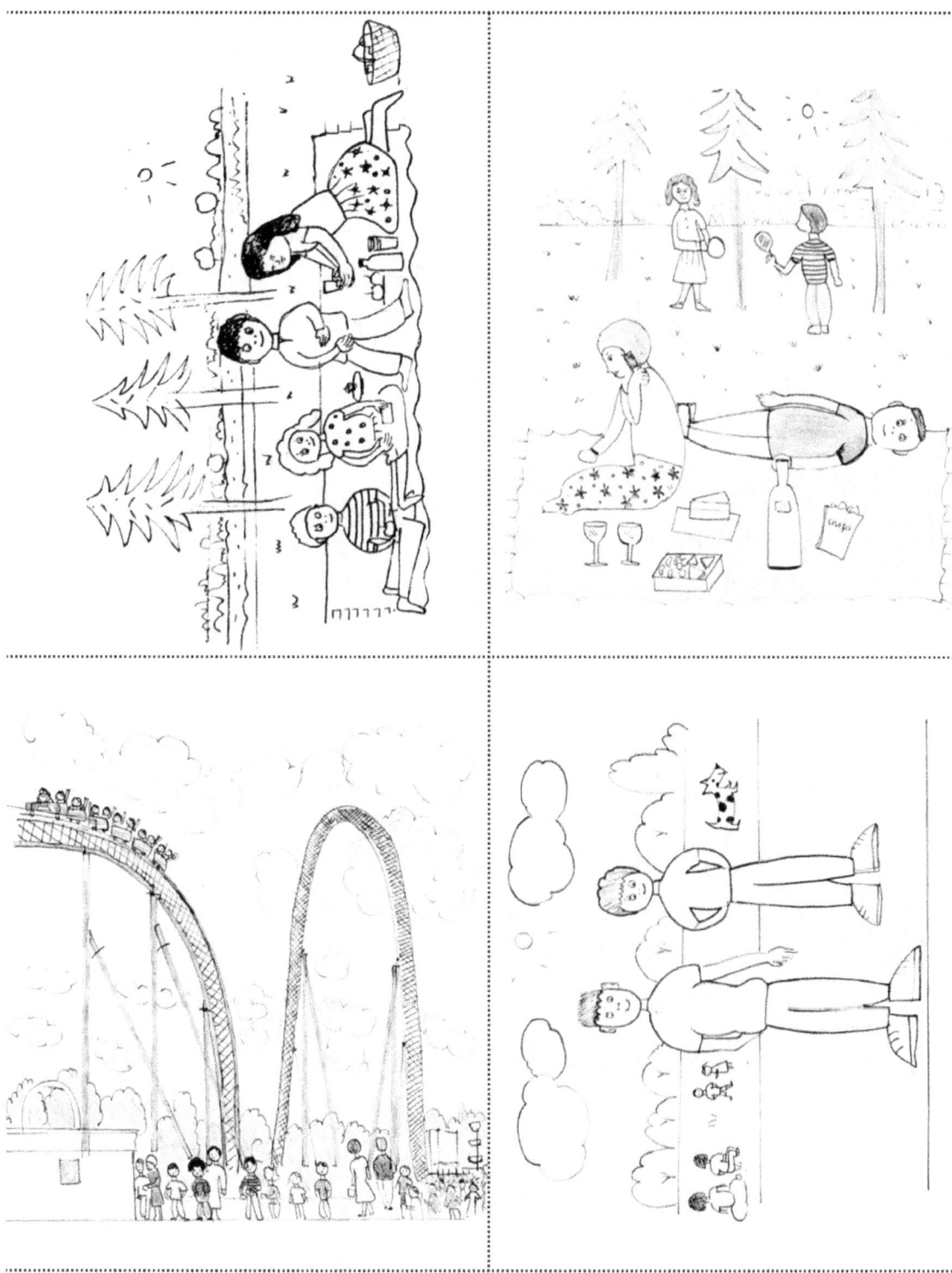

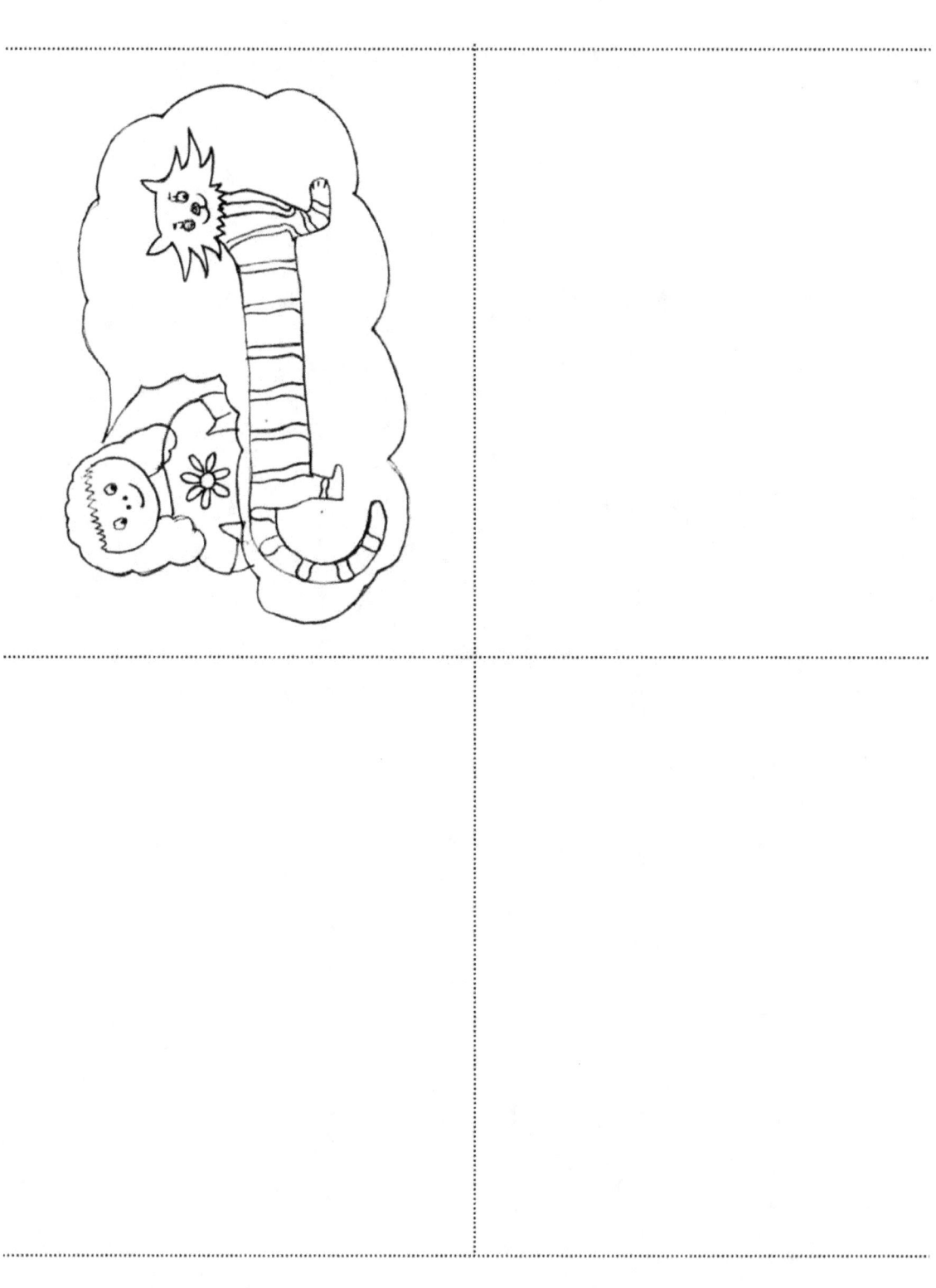

Sally and Amanda Jones

© Copyright 2009

Written by Sally A. Jones and Amanda C. Jones

Published and Printed by GUINEA PIG EDUCATION

2 Cobs Way,
New Haw,
Addlestone, Surrey,
KT15 3AF.
UK.

www.guineapigeducation.co.uk

NO part of this publication may be reproduced, stored or copied for commercial purposes and profit without the prior written permission of the publishers.

ISBN: 978-0-9561150-4-1

Other titles in the Learn To Read With Phonics series include:
Pre-Reader Book 1 ISBN: 978-0-9561150-1-0
Pre-Reader Book 2 ISBN: 978-0-9561150-2-7
Beginner Reader Book 1 ISBN: 978-0-9561150-3-4
Beginner Reader Book 2 ISBN: 978-0-9561150-4-1
Beginner Reader Book 3 ISBN: 978-0-9561150-5-8
Beginner Reader Book 4 ISBN: 978-0-9561150-6-5
Beginner Reader Book 5 ISBN: 978-0-9561150-7-2
Beginner Reader Book 6 ISBN: 978-0-9561150-8-9

www.ingramcontent.com/pod-product-compliance
Lightning Source LLC
Chambersburg PA
CBHW080833010526
44112CB00015B/2506